Preparing for Winter like the Proverbs 31 Woman.

Copyright 2024 paperback edition Christina Fleming

All Rights Reserved. No part of this publication may be reproduced, stored in a retrieval system, or transmitted, in any form or in any means – by electronic, mechanical, photocopying, recording or otherwise – without prior written permission.

Scripture quotations taken from the (NASB®) New American Standard Bible®, Copyright © 1960, 1971, 1977, 1995, by The Lockman Foundation. Used by permission. All rights reserved. www.lockman.org

All photographs and artwork by Christina Fleming.

Distaff and spindle illustration is public domain.

INTRODUCTION

I want to begin by giving a disclaimer: I do not claim to be an expert in this, or any topic. I'm not a Biblical scholar, and while I am college educated, my discipline was not religious studies or theology. What I share in this book is simply my own thoughts on how to prepare for winter like the Proverbs 31 woman. All scripture is taken from the New American Standard Bible.

WHY I WROTE THIS BOOK

In early 2017 I began studying Biblical womanhood, and of course, Proverbs 31 was something I focused on. The woman talked about in verses 10 to 31 is usually seen as one of two things: a role model or something unattainable. She does so many things; she has jobs, raises her family, helps the poor, gardens, sews, invests money, and at the end of it all, her husband and children sing her praises! I have spent a number of years researching this Proverbs 31 woman, and trying to learn how to apply this passage of scripture to my life in present day. Through my study, I determined that it is in fact possible to live like her, but not always in the ways we read.

One passage that stuck out for me was Provers 31:26 which reads *"She is not afraid of the snow for her household, For all her household are clothed with scarlet."*

I began to wonder what this meant, how did she prepare for snow, was her family all wearing red clothing, and so on. Studying this verse in particular inspired me to take an in-depth look at the whole of Proverbs 31 to see what wisdom I can glean when it comes to preparing for winter. How might this accomplished, super homemaker of a woman handle adverse weather with a plan and a level head? That is what I intended to find out. I originally compiled my findings into very short social media posts, but it was hard to edit them all down to be a certain length. I wanted to expand on what I had learned so I decided to write this book.

It is my hope that this book will encourage you to plan ahead for the changing seasons with a Biblical mindset. You do not need any special skills, a lot of money, a specific type of house, or anything like that to benefit from this book. I write for Christian women who are homemakers, but even that term is subjective! If you work full time but still make your home a priority, this book is for you. If you are married with no children, this book is for you. If you are a stay at home mom, this book is for you. Even if you are single, living alone or with family, you can still benefit from this book. Since Proverbs 31 is written about a married woman with children, I will be focussing on that place in life. However, I am not a mother but I still learned a lot while writing this study.

ABOUT ME

Before we get much further, allow me to share a bit more about myself. My husband and I met in college in 2008, and were married in 2012. I've always considered myself a Christian, but in my mid twenties I realized I had a lot of room to improve. I desired to grow closer to God and to be a better wife for my husband, so I began to study scripture more than before. I'm in my thirties now, and am always learning and growing! My husband and I have no children due to infertility, but that does not mean I spend my free time idly. I am a full time homemaker, meaning my job is to care for my husband and our home. Over the years I have maintained a small sewing business, which is a way to have an income on my own schedule. I also run a blog, which I have maintained since 2012. My days are spent cooking, cleaning, organizing the home, planning our social calendars (we are mostly homebodies though!), budgeting and paying bills, sewing, knitting, mending, doing laundry, and whatever tasks are seasonally appropriate. Winter means bringing in firewood and keeping the stoves fed, and summer sees me working in my many vegetable gardens. We enjoy our quiet life on our little homestead with our dog, cat, and chickens. You can connect with me online if you would like.

Blog: www.ourwoodhome.wordpress.com
Instagram: www.instagram.com/our_wood_home
Youtube: www.youtube.com/@ChristinaOurWoodHome

DETAILS ABOUT PROVERBS 31 AND THE BOOK OF PROVERBS IN GENERAL

If you are not overly familiar with Proverbs, or scripture in general, allow me to share some information you may find clarifying. The book of Proverbs is essentially a collection of wisdom and teachings for moral living. We can read about wisdom, what is good for Christian living, what are some things we should avoid, and so on. There are different authors but most of the book was written by King Solomon, but as we read in chapter 31, other Kings and Jewish scholars had their writings included. The sayings and tidbits of wisdom were likely passed down in oral form, from generation to generation, well before King Solomon's time. Additionally, there is some content that was totally new and original for the time.

When we see *Proverbs 31:1* the word indicates which book it is, and the numbers indicate the chapter and verse. The chapter is marked by the first number and the verse is after the colon. I use the New American Standard Bible translation (NASB 1995) so if you are following along in your Bible or reading an online version, the words and phrases may be a little different.

Let's talk about Proverbs 31 in general and what it means for us as modern women. If you are a Christian, you likely already have an opinion about this famed passage of scripture. Surprisingly, many ladies I have spoken to about this were unaware the Proverbs 31 woman didn't actually exist! Most of us are so familiar with verse 10 and onward, but we skip over the first nine. However, if we pay close attention, we learn that the woman written about was not a specific person, but rather a sort of checklist for what a man should look for in a wife. Further, this list was written by his mother! The chapter starts off with a different theme, and that is (in simplified terms) to be a wise and good leader who looks out for the oppressed.

1. The words of King Lemuel, the pronouncement which his mother taught him:

2. What, my son?
And what, son of my womb?
And what, son of my vows?
3. Do not give your strength to women,
Or your ways to that which destroys kings.
4. It is not for kings, Lemuel,
It is not for kings to drink wine,
Or for rulers to desire intoxicating drink,
5. Otherwise they will drink and forget what is decreed,
And pervert the rights of all the needy.
6. Give intoxicating drink to one who is perishing,
And wine to one whose life is bitter.
7. Let him drink and forget his poverty,
And remember his trouble no more.
8. Open your mouth for the people who cannot speak,
For the rights of all the unfortunate.
9. Open your mouth, judge righteously,
And defend the rights of the poor and needy.

Only after all this do we come to the part about the "worthy woman" or "excellent wife", depending on the Bible translation you read.

Description of a Worthy Woman
10 An excellent wife, who can find her?
For her worth is far above jewels.
11 The heart of her husband trusts in her,
And he will have no lack of gain.
12 She does him good and not evil
All the days of her life.
13 She looks for wool and flax,
And works with her hands in delight.
14 She is like merchant ships;
She brings her food from afar.
15 And she rises while it is still night
And gives food to her household,
And portions to her attendants.

*16 She considers a field and buys it;
From her earnings she plants a vineyard.
17 She surrounds her waist with strength
And makes her arms strong.
18 She senses that her profit is good;
Her lamp does not go out at night.
19 She stretches out her hands to the distaff,
And her hands grasp the spindle.
20 She extends her hand to the poor,
And she stretches out her hands to the needy.
21 She is not afraid of the snow for her household,
For all her household are clothed with scarlet.
22 She makes coverings for herself;
Her clothing is fine linen and purple.
23 Her husband is known in the gates,
When he sits among the elders of the land.
24 She makes linen garments and sells them,
And supplies belts to the tradesmen.
25 Strength and dignity are her clothing,
And she smiles at the future.
26 She opens her mouth in wisdom,
And the teaching of kindness is on her tongue.
27 She watches over the activities of her household,
And does not eat the bread of idleness.
28 Her children rise up and bless her;
Her husband also, and he praises her, saying:
29 "Many daughters have done nobly,
But you excel them all."
30 Charm is deceitful and beauty is vain,
But a woman who fears the Lord, she shall be praised.
31 Give her the product of her hands,
And let her works praise her in the gates.*

A SUMMARY OF THE PROVERBS 31 WOMAN

Since the woman described in the above verses was not a living, breathing woman, it is easy to see her way of life as unattainable or exhausting, but there is more to it than that. We can view this as a list of goals for ourselves, something to be constantly working on. Here are the qualities of someone who aspires to be like the Proverbs 31 woman:

- excellent (verse 10)
- trustworthy (verse 11)
- diligent and serving her family using her unique abilities (verses 13-14)
- intentionally runs her household and meets her families needs (verse 15)
- hardworking and makes wise choices (verses 16-18)
- humble and willing to do tasks she doesn't have to do (verse 19)
- has a willingness to serve others (verse 20)
- is prepared and trusts God to meet her needs (verse 21)
- respects herself and her home (verse 22)
- affirms and builds up her family to create a positive home environment (verse 23)
- makes her family a priority over any career (verse 24)
- is strong and dignified; trusts her future to God (verse 25)
- speaks with wisdom and kindness (verse 26)
- is disciplined and intentional with her time (verse 27)
- seeks God's favour above all else (verses 28-29)

Notice how I did not say that to be a modern Proverbs 31 woman we need to all be great cooks, seamstresses, gardeners, or home decorators. Instead, the focus should be on our character and our spiritual disciplines.

With this list in mind, let us delve into how Proverbs 31 can help us prepare for the winter season. Not every single verse in this passage is related to preparedness, but I will still give some notes on them.

HOW TO USE THIS STUDY

I have broken each verse or passage into lessons, for a total of 15 lessons. You can work at your own pace, reading one lesson per day or per week if that suits you. At the end of each lesson there will be some questions or tasks for reflections, if you choose to do it. I hope that you will, because it is going to help you focus in on the application of the verses, and it is a helpful way to track your progress. If you have an extra notebook or just some looseleaf paper, I recommend utilizing that for any notes or to keep track of the reflections. I have left space for writing in this book if you would prefer to do that.

Lesson 1: verse 11

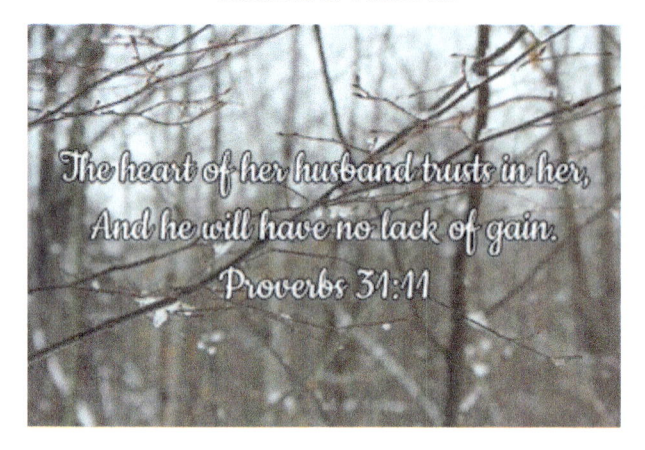

*"The heart of her husband trusts in her,
And he will have no lack of gain."*

What is winter like where you live? Is it cold and snowy, perhaps slightly cooler than summer, is it mostly rainy, or is it hot and dry? Whatever the weather, it is likely different than the seasons preceding it. We can all benefit from making preparations to ensure we are ready for the season and any potentially unexpected surprises. I live in Ontario Canada, in a rural area. Our winters can be all over the place, from bitterly cold to mild and slushy. But with winter (in any form) comes power outages, bad driving conditions, and varied weather. My husband trusts that I will stay on top of things so that we are safe and prepared.

Trustworthiness is a quality the Proverbs 31 woman possesses as seen in verse 11. What exactly does it mean to be trustworthy? According to multiple dictionaries it can be defined in the following ways:

- sound judgement
- genuine concerns for another's well being
- faithful
- someone who can be relied on

These are from secular dictionaries, but I noticed all of those traits that can be used to describe a person can ALSO be said of God. If we want to be imitators of God (as we are told in Ephesians 5:1-2), I'd say that we should be aiming to have the qualities that make us trustworthy.

Are you trustworthy in the eyes of your husband? There may be some of you reading this who are thinking "my husband trusts nobody, certainly not me!". I acknowledge many people have had experiences that negatively affect their ability to trust people. In situations like that, even close family or friends are often hard to trust, even if they have proven trustworthy. I do not want to downplay those very real issues, but I am not qualified to speak on them any further. For the sake of this study, let us focus on what it means for us as wives to be trustworthy and why that is relevant to winter preparations.

Firstly, as a wife (and maybe mother, grandmother, or guardian of children) our role is to be the keeper of our homes. Let's not spend time debating whether or not wives and mothers should have jobs, but instead agree that our priority needs to be our family. We will read later the Proverbs 31 woman seems to have a job in some capacity, and there are other women in scripture who work. But as we will see with the rest of this study, our focus needs to be on our family. Our ultimate priority as Christians should be God, followed by our spouse and then children. While our duties as homemaker/keeper of the home may vary from woman to woman, the management of our household should be primarily our responsibility. Our families rely on us to make sure there is food to prepare, meals to eat, clean clothes to wear, and so on. That does not mean we have to be the one to do all those things, and delegating is a valuable skill to have as a keeper of the home! I am not so naive to think there are some families in which the husband does a lot of the house work or cooking or chores. But for the duration of this study I will be emphasizing the importance of wives running their homes.

A trustworthy woman is someone her family can depend on. She is someone who keeps her word, knows how to control her tongue, is reliable, can be a comfort to others in time of need, and is discreet.
Being trustworthy like the Proverbs 31 woman during the time of winter preparations means we are making sure our family is equipped for the changing seasons. It means they rightfully rely on to keep them fed, warm, and safe to the best of our abilities.

Reflection Questions:

1. Read through Proverbs 31:10-31 and note any character traits that stand out to you. Are there any you already observe in yourself? Which traits are goals of yours?

2. Pray for a humble spirit willing to learn. You can use the example prayer below if you are unsure what to say.

3. Pray for wisdom as you prepare for the winter. You can use the example prayer below if you are unsure what to say.

Prayer for a humble and willing spirit:
Dear Lord, I ask that You would give me a humble spirit that is willing to learn as I work through this study. Soften my heart so I may be made aware of any behaviours I need to work on, and show me ways to improve. Amen

Prayer for wisdom:
Dear Lord, please give me wisdom as I work on preparing my family and home for the upcoming winter. Show me ways to serve my family and how to anticipate our needs. Amen

Lesson 2: verse 12

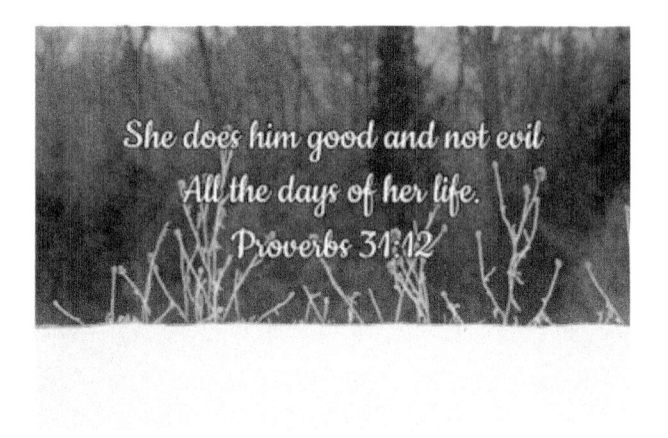

*"She does him good and not evil
All the days of her life."*

Verse 12 does not specifically relate to winter but it is still worth mentioning. As we did in lesson 1, let's establish some definitions. The word good is something we can all use clearly and properly, but here are some ways it can be defined:

- adjective: to be desired or approved of
- adjective: that can be relied on
- noun: that which is morally right; righteous
- noun: benefit or advantage to someone or something
- noun: advancement of prosperity or well-being

The word evil is another word that can be defined easily:

- morally bad or wrong; wicked; depraved

All the various online dictionaries used similar wording and phrases to define evil, so I summarized with this one.

Based on the definitions for both words, how can be we translate Proverbs 31:12 into modern day, and for winter preparations specifically?

Think back to lesson 1, in which we read about being trustworthy. Two of the definitions used are "genuine concerns for another's well being" and "someone who can be relied on". Being trustworthy means we look out for the interests of others and have proven to be dependable. To do our husband good means we are taking care of him and looking out for his well-being by planning ahead. By that standard, the opposite would be to do him evil by NOT ensuring he is prepared for winter. I know, that may sound like an overreach, and I am not trying to imply that you are an evil person if you do not cater to your husband. What I am saying is that it is so important for wives to do what they can to help their husbands in any situation. I do not have a full time, for pay job, but that doesn't mean I am not contributing to our household. The ways I help my husband include taking care of seasonal preparations, including those listed in this book, so that he has less to worry about.

While verse 12 does not give us specific tasks for winter prep, we can still use it as motivation.

Reflection Questions:

1. Make a list of ways you can do your husband good in anticipation of winter. Keep this list handy for reference throughout the rest of the study.

2. Read the following Bible verses for more insights about doing good: Proverbs 14:1, Proverbs 12:1, Proverbs 19:14, Proverbs 21:9.

Lesson 3: verse 13

*"She looks for wool and flax,
And works with her hands in delight."*

Most of us probably know that wool comes from animals, but how much do you know about flax? Prior to doing research for this study, I knew flax is a flowering plant that looks spindly and has small blueish purple flowers. I also knew flaxseed is high in fibre and can be used to replicate eggs in vegan cooking. However, I was not aware that flax in the context of this verse was used for clothing! Put in very simplistic terms, the flax plant stalks are very fibrous and that is what is used for making fabrics. Of course, there is much more to it than that, but it is not entirely relevant to this study, but still very interesting. When flax is harvested, dried, and woven into cloth, we get linen. It is a very lightweight, yet sturdy fabric.

 In Biblical times all garments were made from either wool or linen. Wool was used in heavier fabrics for colder weather, and for garments such as coats, while linen was typically a warmer weather fabric. Additionally linen was used to make garments worn directly against the skin but they could also be layered.

The Proverbs 31 woman makes sure her family is ready for all weather, and with all types of clothing, by actively looking for the materials needed. The words "looks for" in verse 13 indicate the care she took in finding these materials. She didn't grab the first thing she saw, or pick whatever was cheapest. No, she made an effort to look for good quality wool and flax. Maybe that means she literally examined different animals for their wool, or went to the weavers to see the raw materials. Maybe it means she went to the markets and examined all the finished garments thoroughly before committing to purchases. When we read the phrase "she works", this means she is purposefully seeking ways to provide for her family in the ways she is able. Many women were skilled fabric weavers, but that doesn't mean everyone was. Just like in present day, some ladies are still skilled weavers, seamstresses, knitters, or crocheters, while lots of others do not have those skills. Our Proverbs 31 lady doesn't have to be the finest weaver, so perhaps she would hire someone to do that part. But even if that is the scenario, she would still be very diligent and thorough in seeking out garment makers. She would not choose the cheapest option if it was also poor quality.

How does this apply to us as we prepare for winter?

We certainly should not expect ourselves to seek out raw materials and make clothes for our family! Nor does it mean we should all be sewing or knitting/crocheting everything we wear. If you want to, that is fine, but it is not practical for most.

What this verse means for us is that we should be ensuring our family has the appropriate clothing for winter, whatever that means for us. In my household we wear heavy coats, knit hats, mittens, scarves, and boots in winter. My husband works outside for his job, so he needs to wear certain gloves that allow for dexterity, and toques that can fit under a hard hat. Sometimes he wears snow pants or hip waders too. When he snowplows our driveway he wears a different set of winter accessories. Part of my job as keeper of the home is to make sure all my husband's seasonal gear (and my own!) is in good repair. If his coat has a tear in the pocket, I can easily mend it. If the gloves have been separated I will look for them to make a pair (or buy a new pair if needed). His snow pants have a hole that is beyond repair so that means I am looking for a new pair to buy that is good quality and well priced (and I do this now before he needs them). These are not tasks my husband asks of me, but I know they need to be done so I am doing them proactively. And while doing so I am not complaining about how he needs to be careful not to lose his gloves; I am happy to do these things because it is part of taking care of my household. Like the Proverbs 31 woman does, I want to be intentionally and thoughtfully do my part to meet the needs of my family.

Of course, if you live in a climate that does not have snow, your winter needs will be different. Even if the only wardrobe changes you need to make are a light jacket and some closed toe shoes, you can still follow this lesson and do the reflection questions (perhaps with modifications).

Reflection Questions:

1. Take time to sort through all the winter coats, boots, hats, etc in your home looking for anything that is not in good condition. If it can be repaired, set it aside, and if it is beyond repair, throw it out (if it is in good shape but is no longer used or does not fit, donate it).

2. Set aside time to fix the items that need care. You can enlist the help of family members to wash all the coats, waterproof the boots, sew on buttons, etc. Do not feel you need to do every task by yourself.

3. If you need to purchase new items, make a list of what you need and begin sourcing replacements. If the budget allows, purchase items before the winter weather hits, otherwise they may not be as available or have increased in price.

Lesson 4: verse 14

*"She is like the merchant ships;
She brings her food from afar."*

When you think of this verse, what comes to mind? Do you imagine the Proverbs 31 lady carrying back arms full of exotic foods and spices? Maybe she buys the most expensive foods she can find, or maybe she travels a far distance to get new foods for her family. Does this mean we are to be actively seeking out fancy or interesting meal ingredients or driving all across town to specialty grocery stores?

Those are plausible ideas, but my research shows a different story. Think about a big cargo ship: does it make good sense for a cargo ship to journey if it is only partially full? More than likely a cargo ship is going to be fully loaded, making the most of its trip. It might take different kinds of goods, but when it starts its journey, it is full and efficient.

In the time the Bible was written, merchant ships would bring in items that were not available in the immediate area, and people would be able to purchase them. Perhaps the Proverbs 31 woman sells woven garments (verse 13) and uses the profits to buy special and exotic foods from these merchant ships? If so, that would indicate her willingness to use her talents to support her family. Comparing her to a merchant ship could also mean that she actively seeks ways and places to sell her goods for a profit.

There is a second potential interpretation of this verse, and that is that she is actively seeking interesting and healthy foods for her family's meals. Ships are not a fast moving vehicle, they are slow and take their time to reach their destination. They are loaded with items, since it would not be practical to partially fill them and then make many more trips. Perhaps the comparison of this woman to a merchant ship is meant to be taken as a form of encouragement for modern homemakers. Like ships, we should take our time to make healthy and tasty meals for our family. I know it is so easy to load your grocery cart with frozen pizzas, soups in a can, and heat and serve meals. And there is nothing wrong with those on occasion but we, as homemakers, should be taking the time and effort and making a self sacrifice to prepare home cooked meals to the best of our means.

Yes, I said sacrifice! In Ephesians 5:1-2 it says to be an imitator of God, and walk in love as Jesus did. Jesus sacrificed Himself for us, so surely we can make a few sacrifices in our own life! I mean, I would quite enjoy sitting on the couch reading a good book all day, but I know that there are other important things to do around the house. I am sacrificing or giving up something I want in order to serve the needs of my husband.

To prepare for winter like the Proverbs 31 woman we can make sure we get a handle on meal planning, grocery shopping, and food storage. Please do not feel like you need to preplan every meal your family will eat for the next 3 months! If that is something you want to do, go ahead, but that is likely not very realistic for most of us.

We can all do some form of meal planning though. You can start by thinking about any upcoming holiday feasts, and make a list of what you would like to serve. As your grocery budget allows, you can start purchasing ingredients in advance of the holidays. Maybe you can decide that every Friday in the winter will be a "build your own bowl of chilli" for dinner, using inexpensive ingredients such as rice and beans as the base. Perhaps every Sunday you will serve a meatless lunch. Whatever you choose to do, it can be beneficial to have some rough idea of meals you would like to make over winter. If you prefer to stick to the same types of foods and not try much variety, that is okay too! I would suggest confirming with your family to make sure they are on board with that idea though. It can be a little monotonous to eat only a small variety of meals. Let's say you prefer to make soups and stews primarily. Maybe you can experiment with some new vegetables to add in, or try some different herbs and spices. Perhaps offer some tasty crackers or bread alongside the soup.

You do not need to be a gourmet chef, always trying new recipes, but consider coming up with some type of plan for meals. This will also help you stay on budget since you will be buying what you need, and not random ingredients.

Let's talk about grocery shopping: how often do you make trips to the store? Consider less frequent trips if possible, to save on gas and on time. Also if possible, try to go to the fewest amount of stores instead of driving all over town. I know some people do this to save on products at each store, but you are likely spending more on gas driving all over, therefore cancelling out any grocery savings. When you shop, make sure you have a list! Keep your list somewhere convenient in the house so you can easily add to it when you run out of something.

I do not support food hoarding, but I think we can all benefit from some form of long or short term food stockpile. If you live in an area with extreme weather, you may not be able to get to a grocery store for a few days, so you want to make sure you have enough food to last. Likewise, if you are in an extended power outage you will want to have foods that require minimal preparation. It might be worth the investment to buy a propane powered camp stove, which you can use outside during a power outage for heating up meals.

If power outages are a possibility, consider how you will feed and hydrate your family. If you are on well water, your pump is likely electric so it will not operate in an outage. If you have the resources, I suggest doing some research on canning potable water for emergencies. You simply need canning jars and lids! Alternatively, you can purchase some jugs of water and keep them sealed until you need them. In a snowy climate there is the option of collecting, melting, and boiling snow to drink, but you need to have some way to boil it. We use our wood stove but I would much prefer to simply open a jug or jar of drinkable water! Think about some foods that are easy to prepare and eat without power. Canned soups (store bought or home canned) are great in an emergency, but only if you have a way to heat them. Tinned tuna and crackers makes a quick and easy meal, dried fruit is a nice snack, and sandwiches make a good dinner in a pinch.

Living in Canada, where the winters can be quite cold, means we have the option to store food outside in a power outage. The freezing temperatures will help prevent food from spoiling, but this is not an ideal situation. We have a small generator that we can connect to our fridge and freezers if needed. If you are able, I suggest looking into purchasing one for your home. It might be pricey but a worthwhile investment.

I highly recommend canning food as an alternative to freezing, whenever possible. Canning is not scary, but it does require care and attention, as well as some specialty equipment. You will need canning jars and appropriate lids, as well as a water bath canner or pressure canner, depending on what you want to can. Meat and most vegetables need to be pressure canned, but things like jams and pickles do not. There are a lot of great canning resources online, so do your research. It is best to follow expert advice from sources such as Ball Canning, Healthy Canning, Bernardin, or if you live in America you can contact your local extension office.

Meal planning, efficient grocery shopping, and food storage can sound intimidating but I hope you give it a try, even if you take baby steps. Having some type of plan in place will help you be more prepared for winter.

Reflection Questions:

1. Come up with a list of shelf stable foods that can be prepared or served easily in a power outage (canned fish, dry crackers, dried fruit bars, minute rice, etc).

2. Create a list of pantry or freezer staples you would like to always keep on hand. This could be canned soup, frozen vegetables, certain spices, tea, etc.

3. Using your two lists from above, start grocery shopping for your regular items but also to create a small stockpile.

4. Consider planning out winter meals now. What holidays need to be accounted for? Include those food items in your plan.

5. Research canning methods and decide if it is something you want to start doing.

Lesson 5: verse 15

*"She rises while it is still night
And gives food to her household,
And portions to her attendants."*

There are about 70 countries in the world that recognize daylight savings time (DST) in at least some areas, so chances are you live in one of those countries! Although, at the time of writing this book there have been talk of Canada and America doing away with it altogether, but it has not happened yet. With DST in effect it might look like the middle of the night when you get up in the morning! But are we to take verse Proverbs 31:15 literally and begin our day while it is not even technically daytime yet? Biblical scholars tell us that this passage does not mean literal nighttime, between sunset and sunrise, but is meant to illustrate simply starting the day early.

The Proverbs 31 woman is willing and ready to get things going. She desires to be productive and knows it is more achievable if she has a head start on the day. I realize waking up early may not be feasible for many women, for a variety of reasons, so let's not make the time we arise the focus here. If the word early means 5:00 AM for you, great. And if it means 7:00 AM, also great.

Oh, how I love to try to sleep in, especially since I usually have chronic insomnia. It would be so much easier, and more comfortable, and dare I say, even thoughtful if my husband David would let me sleep in. He could get up early to prepare for his day...then he could make his own lunch and breakfast too. While he is up, he can take extra time to care for the chickens, let the dog out, and build the fires in the wood stove. I mean, it would just be SO THOUGHTFUL of him to let me rest a bit more.

Did you pick up on the sarcasm there?

It certainly would be nice for that to happen, but it would be even nicer if I was the one doing what I can to make my husband's day run smoother. He works hard all day so that I am able to stay a homemaker. When I wake up at a reasonable time, I feel like I'm contributing to a better day for David, because his pre-work tasks are minimal. When I get a head start on my share of the morning tasks, he knows he won't be rushed or late leaving because everything else is taken care of.

Let's talk about the latter half of this verse. My first thought about "household" and "attendants" was in reference to hired help. That doesn't apply to me, and maybe not many of you either. I did some research, and there were a few different ideas as to what this means. Firstly, it could literally mean this woman cares for the needs of her staff and makes sure they are ready to begin their days. If that is the case, she is a very thoughtful employer! How does that translate to us as present day keepers of the home? I suppose if you have hired help for cleaning, cooking, child care, etc, it could mean that you treat them with respect and utmost appreciation. Doing so would show that you care about the needs of people you aren't required to care for. If you don't have household staff, you can still learn from this passage. It indicates that we should be selfless, caring for others, thinking about people we may otherwise take for granted.

The other interpretation I came across was that household means her family. Her husband and children, and whomever else may be related to her and living in that dwelling. So this wife and mother gets up early to make sure that her family's needs are met, maybe even before her own. She serves her family, actively pursues ways to meet their needs, and does so with intent and happiness. Part of making that happen is starting our days with purpose and a diligent spirit. It means we make our family a priority.

I don't want to be misinterpreted, though. My words aren't meant to be read as *"women should put themselves last at all times, and make sure their husband and kids have everything they need first."* Doing so all the time can cause burnout, stress, resentment, and even physical health problems. When I get up early to help my husband I make sure my basic needs are met first (bathroom, tidy my hair so it is out of my way, get a quick drink or snack if I need it, etc). The point I am trying to make is that we, as wives who aspire to be like the Proverbs 31 woman, should be making an effort to care for the needs of our families.

I want us all to honestly think about our morning routines. Are we slow to get out of bed, perhaps even lazy? Do we hastily throw together breakfast for our husband and he runs off to work? Do the kids have to fend for themselves for their first meal of the day? Are we sleeping in late and feeling unproductive throughout the day? Maybe we need to reread Proverbs 31:15 and think about what it means for us.

Here are some practical ways to apply this scripture to our lives as we prepare for winter:

• Waking up early enough to assist the rest of our family with starting their day.
• Preparing breakfast (things like overnight oats, fruit salad, pre-made muffins or breakfast sandwiches) or packing lunches the night before .
• Going to bed at a reasonable time so we are not exhausted in the morning.
• Getting up 10 minutes earlier than usual to spend time in prayer for our family (for safety in travel to school or work, to make wise choices throughout the day, for patience in each member if everyone is home together, etc).

It can be a struggle to wake up early, and each of us has to decide what that means for her. To me, "early" in the winter means before 6:00 AM, as I am usually out of bed around 6:30. As mentioned before, there are many reasons a woman might not be able to get up early (working late, health problems, etc), but it should not be an excuse for not trying to live out this verse in Proverbs. We should not come to this with the mindset of "well, I have to be up late to get the house cleaned up and the lunches packed, so I deserve to sleep in. Everyone can take care of themselves in the morning." Preparing for each day in the previous evening may be of help, and if there are older children in the home, they can assist the younger in the morning. Do not look for ways to get out of preparing like the Proverbs 31 woman (I recognize things like chronic illness, fussy babies, and more can play a role in poor sleeping and waking habits but I would encourage you to still aim to follow this study in all aspects as you are able).

Let us all aim to be more productive in the mornings, however we can!

Reflection Questions:

1. Identify any struggles you have or areas that are lacking efficiency within your morning routine. For example, is it hard for you to wake up, do you feel too rushed in the morning, are you staying up late scrolling social media?

2. Come up with solutions to remedy the problems of point 1 (ex: making breakfast the night before, going to bed earlier, having a cool shower to help wake you up first thing in the morning, laying out clothes the night before, setting your alarm and placing the clock or phone across the room, etc).

3. Commit to spending 5 minutes in the morning praying for your family. This can be while you shower, pack lunches, make the bed, or during devotional time. Increase that time when you feel ready.

Lesson 6: verse 16

*"She considers a field and buys it;
From her earnings she plants a vineyard."*

Verse 15 tells us the Proverbs 31 woman CONSIDERS a field, meaning she takes her time to think about what she is buying. It also tells us the following:

- this woman is financially wise and has extra means for large purchases
- the word <u>considers</u> indicates her ability to think critically and thoughtfully before making rash decisions
- the field she purchases makes her a profit, because she made a smart purchase of land that was able to produce well; then she turns around and plants an even more profitable crop

This verse may seem like it doesn't apply to us, especially as we prepare for winter, but I assure you it does! Now, I don't know about you, but my husband would not be happy if I told him I bought a field (or farm). He would wonder how I physically did that because I wouldn't qualify for a mortgage and I don't have a small fortune tucked away. We make decisions together, so doing something like making a large purchase on my own seems a bit weird. Is this portion of scripture telling us women that we can do that? I do not believe so.   Let's take a look back at verse 11: *the heart of her husband trusts in her, and he will have no lack of gain.* This woman has proven trustworthy, and her husband is confident in giving her a portion of their family income to do as she sees fit. He knows that she will make wise spending choices and he respects her financial investment decisions. When she spends or invests, she takes her time and is confident in her choices. She looks ahead and plans accordingly, and isn't afraid of hard work, because she knows she is capable. Verse 15 reminds us to be wise with our finances.

Not everyone is in the position to make investments, and not every wife is in charge of the family finances. I do all the budgeting and bill payments, but my husband is the one with investment accounts, which he opened before we were married. Due to tax reasons I am not listed on his accounts so I can't make any decisions about them. But if I wanted to, I can do some research on different types of investments, provide him with the information, and he can talk it over with the investor. I do recognize that having any type of savings or investments is not the norm for a lot of people, so I will not focus on that in this lesson. Instead we will hone in on being financially wise and trustworthy.

I have noticed there seem to be more expenses but usually less funds in the winter months, so I need to do my best to manage the household budget well.

For me this means:
- doing some meal planning so I can smartly use our grocery funds on what we need
- deciding on Christmas gifts early on and saving accordingly (also picking items for loved ones that are within our budget!)
- resisting the urge to online shop out of boredom

What does it mean for you? Maybe it means reusing winter clothes, shopping second-hand for things you need, planning budget friendly meals, or setting spending limits for holiday gifts.

The latter half of verse 15 says she plants a vineyard from her profits. We don't have to start investing our money to emulate this scripture, but we should remember to plan ahead. A vineyard takes time to grow and become established, so the Proverbs 31 woman demonstrates to us her capability to plan for the future. She is not simply living in the moment! Let us use verse 15 to remind us that we are to use funds wisely, be confident in our decision making, and to work hard at whatever job we have. The Proverbs 31 woman was clearly a hard worker, and while it may seem like she had a job outside the home, we can still emulate her as full time homemakers or stay at home mothers.

Reflection Questions:

1. What are some ways you can manage your budget a little better? Write them down as goals. Talk to your husband about it as well, and get his opinion. Be willing to make some sacrifices to get to your budgetary goals.

2. Start planning ahead for winter by getting some extra groceries (as we discussed in lesson 5), filling up portable gas can for the snow blower, buying extra mittens for the kids, organizing your family's board games for those "I'm bored" days. Of course, these are just suggestions! Think of some things that would make yours, and your family's, life easier this winter and work on implementing them.

Lesson 7: verses 17-18

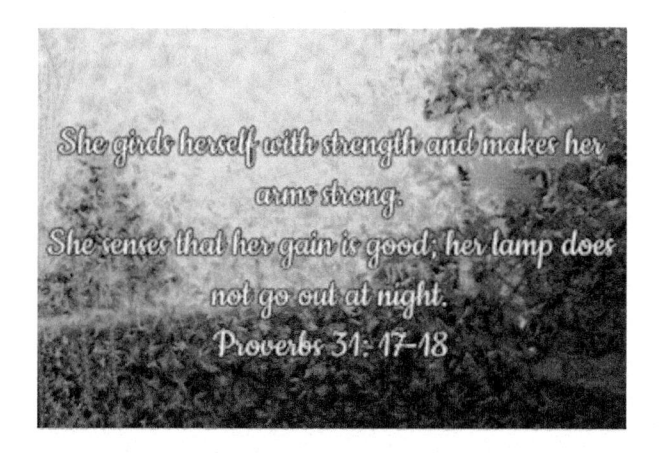

*"She girds herself with strength and makes her arms strong.
She senses that her gain is good; her lamp does not go out at night."*

What is your personal definition of "strong"? Does it mean you can bench press a certain amount, can lift your children as much as they need it, are able to push a stuck car out of a ditch, can you carry all the groceries in yourself? Whatever it means to you, surely we all desire to have some bodily strength. In order to be strong we generally need to be in good health. This means we get enough sleep (easier said than done maybe!), drink enough water, have healthy eating habits, and stay active. Once again, I realize this may not be possible for everyone. In 2021 I had an injury that resulted in loss of strength that I am still trying to build up again. I also suffer from chronic migraines and chronic back/hip pain which makes life in general difficult. I am fully aware that some readers may be unable to do much physical labour or they struggle to maintain healthy eating habits. I still believe we can all benefit from this lesson and can implement the Reflection Questions in some way.

One of my winter responsibilities is shovelling off our front and back steps when it snows. This is hard for me to do because of how easily I can strain my back, but it helps if I maintain my stretching routine all season. I am also responsible for starting the wood stove fires, which usually means I bring in firewood as well. My husband and I share the duties of letting our dog out to do her business and tending the chickens. My body could not handle that much physical work if I ate junky food and did not do any form of regular exercise. I desire to be productive at home and contribute in the ways I am able, so this verse serves as a good reminder to keep my physical body in shape.

Some other translations of scripture say she girds her loins, and the word gird means to tuck up the hem of your long garment into your belt or waistband to keep it out of the way; this was done when hard work was expected.

The woman of Proverbs 31 is ready to get involved in all manner of tasks and she kept herself in good physical shape to do so. She did not play into the old stereotype of women being weak and helpless; she used the strength she had to do tasks she needed to do. We know from verse 14 that meals were important and healthy whenever possible, and this shows a preparedness. Winter often brings difficult tasks for us, and we should be willing, as we are able, to conquer them. It can be so easy to fall into bad habits when it is cold out! We may want to eat more comfort foods, which are not going to strengthen our bodies. We may find ourselves spending more time indoors on the couch and the very idea of going for a walk is unappealing. I can defiantly sympathize with that because I've experienced those same things. But as I mentioned earlier in this lesson, I desire to be a contributing member of this household and to do so, I need to be in good health.

Moving onto verse 18, we see a reminder of the previous lesson about about making good financial choices. Now we read the Proverbs 31 is confident in her choices (*"her gain is good"*) and that she continues to work hard (*"her lamp does not go out at night"*). We certainly do not need to be staying up all hours of the night working on various household tasks. But similarly to verse 15 about rising while it is still night, we can be reminded to work hard and diligently. Instead of flopping onto the couch or bed as soon as our evening meal is finished, let us be in a preparedness mindset. How can we prepare for tomorrow today? What will make our day easier and smoother? It could be that folding laundry tonight will give you more time for other tasks tomorrow, so turn on a podcast or TV show and get folding. If you load up the dirty dishes into the dishwasher now, you can wake up to a tidy kitchen. I am a big fan of listening to music or a Christian teaching podcast while I do work because it makes things feel less drawn out.

By keeping ourselves in good shape and maintaining healthy habits, we give ourselves the ability to be productive and prepared for winter. If you have finished the study up until now, hopefully you can sense that your gain is good as you work towards being more prepared for winter.

Reflection Questions:

1. Make some health goals for the winter, and start implementing them now. This could mean doing some form of exercise for 10 minutes each day, reducing your sugar intake, cooking more homemade meals, going to sleep earlier, etc.

2. Write out a personal mission statement for your role as a wife, homemaker, mother, or caregiver. Put it somewhere you will see it often and read it when you need a reminder to work diligently. I have included my homemaking mission statement to give you an idea.

homemaking mission statement

I am blessed to be the keeper of my home.
I will joyfully and faithfully serve my family to the best of my abilities.
My home will be one of peace, joy, and love, that is welcoming to others.

Lesson 8: verse 19

*"She stretches out her hands to the distaff,
And her hands grasp the spindle."*

If you read this verse and have no idea what it is talking about, you are not alone! A distaff and spindle are used for spinning raw fibres, such as wool or flax, into a finished thread that can be used for weaving (remember we read about wool and flax in lesson 3). The raw materials are wrapped around the distaff and when they are spun, they are stored on the spindle. There are different ways to go about spinning using these tools, but I want you to to notice something about the illustration below.

In this example it shows the woman using both her hands instead of one. That is important, but we will come back to that.

We have to remember that Proverbs 31 is written as advice from a mother to her son, King Lemuel. So why would a future queen need to make her own clothing? Surely she would have the finest weavers and garments makers at her disposal, right? Perhaps this is meant to show us that the Proverbs 31 woman is:

· humble
· hard working
· willing to do things she doesn't really have to
· diligent

Those all sounds like traits we can embrace as modern day women. But if God wanted us to simply glean those things from this passage, why the reference to spinning? Take a look at Exodus 35:25-26.

All the skilled women spun with their hands, and brought what they had spun, in blue and purple and scarlet material and in fine linen. All the women whose heart stirred with a skill spun the goat's hair.

When the tabernacle was being built people contributed how they could. Some worked with wood, others used various metals or stones, and so on. From reading the earlier verses in Exodus 35 is appears to me that people of wealth or higher class brought costly goods because that is what they had to give. Then the working people contributed labour or whatever skills they had. So the women doing the spinning were regular women, not really of noble class or anything like that. But clearly it was an important task!

All of that is interesting, but still does not answer the question of WHY the Proverbs 31 woman (who is the ideal wife for a king) would need to be skilled in spinning! It is seemingly a commoner task.

Look back to the image I shared showing how a distaff and spindle are used. And then let's read Proverbs 31:19 again:

*She stretches out her hands to the distaff,
And her hands grasp the spindle.*

It clearly states that she uses her hands, both hands, not just one. Using these tools in this way means the user is not idly sitting around, being lazy or unproductive. If we read further in verse 27 of Proverbs 31 we see that this woman doesn't eat the bread of idleness. She looks for ways to use her time well, so perhaps THAT is what we can learn from verse 19. In biblical days there were no toilets to scrub, socks to match, schedules to coordinate, homeschool curriculum to be planned, sports practices to rush to, but this verse is teaching us that wives should be domestically skilled in whatever tasks are appropriate for their family. You don't have to be the best chef or have the most organized home, but you should be making an effort to keep your home running in good order.

Spinning raw fibres is a skill that took time to master, and was a very useful one to have. A woman who could spin showed that she had dedication, was willing to work hard, and was not lazy.

As we prepare for winter we can be inspired by this verse, and make sure we are not allowing ourselves to become idle. When it is cold outside it can be very tempting to wrap myself up in blankets and read a book or watch movies all day. But that would be giving into idleness, and that is not God-honouring behaviour. Of course, there are days when we all need a break or a rest and it is important to do so, but we need to still remember our role as keeper of the home. In lesson 3 of our study the Reflection Questions was to work on meal planning or at least having a good supply of pantry/freezer foods. This will come in handy on days we don't feel like cooking!

Here are my personal tips for when I am feeling lazy and idle:
· set a timer for 20 minutes and spend that time cleaning
· put on some upbeat music
· do a boring chore like folding laundry or ironing while watching a short YouTube video or listening to a podcast
· give myself permission to stop housework at 4:00 to allow for some rest time before dinner (this gives me a set time frame for work, so it makes it more doable)

Reflection Questions:

1. Pray asking God to show you any ways you have been lazy in your role as keeper of the home. Use the example prayer below if you are struggling to find the words.

Prayer to be convicted of lazy behaviours:

Dear Lord, please show me how I have been lazy or idle in my duties as homemaker. I want to be more productive in my home so please give me motivation, and when I start feeling lazy, stir something in me. Amen.

2. Consider asking a member of your household to keep you accountable as you work on any lazy habits. You could also ask a friend or family member who doesn't live with you.

3. Try setting a timer for cleaning. Do it once a day for a few days and then slowly increase the time. This can help end a laziness slump.

Lesson 9, verse 20

*"She extends her hand to the poor,
And she stretches out her hands to the needy."*

Have you heard the phrase "blessed to be a blessing"? The idea behind it is that God has blessed us in so many ways, and we should be blessing others in the ways we are able. This is an especially nice thing to do during the holiday season, as is often seen with the myriad of charitable giving campaigns. The city near us hosts a toy drive at various stores and businesses, and asks the community to donate a new toy for children in the foster care system. My local food bank seeks seasonal food donations to create special meal kits for low income families. Even some nursing homes put together wish lists for their residents, and community members can play secret Santa. These are just some of the programs offered where I live, and you can likely find something similar near you. While it is nice to give or participate in holiday charity, it is something we can practice all year. I'm choosing to include this topic in our winter preparedness study because typically people are more likely to donate during the Christmas season, which occurs in winter here in the Northern Hemisphere.

You might be thinking you would like to donate to charity but it is not in the budget. That is another reason I included this topic, because we can start planning and setting some money aside now. Regardless of income, everyone can likely find a cause they feel passionate about donating to! As we get into winter, let us take a cue from the Proverbs 31 woman, who is:

- humble
- hard working
- willing to do things she doesn't really have to
- diligent
- thoughtful
- wise

She certainly cares about helping those who are less fortunate, and as Christians, we should too! Here are some ways we can extend our hand to the poor, and stretch out our hands to the needy:

• helping deliver meals to shut ins or the sick
• assisting an elderly neighbour with yard work
• offering shuttle service for cancer patients (there is an organization locally that offers this free of charge for people needing treatment in the larger city near us)
• picking up a few extra groceries or personal care items when you shop to donate to a food bank

- knitting or crocheting hats, blankets, booties, etc for premature babies in the hospital
- organizing or volunteering with a baby item drive for a local crisis pregnancy centre
- creating handmade cards for veterans or military personnel
- donating new blankets and bedding to animal shelters
- sponsoring a family for Christmas through local charities
- volunteering time at the food bank (they often need help sorting items)
- donating new items to nursing homes (contact them first to see what they need, but here are some ideas: puzzles, word search books, DVDs for residents to watch, wall calendars, cozy socks, lap blankets, yarn for knitting or crochet)
- donating new mittens and hats to the local public schools for children who lose or forget theirs (or don't have any to begin with)

While it is true that some of these ideas do require you to spend money, there are many ways that only require time. If it is appropriate to do so, you could involve your children in some of the tasks as well. If you homeschool, perhaps you can use this as part of their social studies or civics lesson. If you do not celebrate Christmas, you can still get involved in the community before or after the holiday.

Remember the Proverbs 31 woman would not be a self seeking person. She would not take photos volunteering to show how charitable she was. She would not post on Facebook that she would be donating a month's salary to a homeless shelter. She doesn't help people because she wants the attention, she does it because she sees the need and wants to meet it.

Reflection Questions:

1. Discuss as a family if you are financially able to bless someone else this winter. It does not have to be a Christmas blessing, it can be anytime! If financial support is not possible, consider other ways to be a blessing.

2. What causes are you passionate about? Look for community organizations that you can donate time, money, or resources to.

Lesson 10, verse 21

*"She is not afraid of the snow for her household,
For all her household are clothed with scarlet."*

As we continue preparing for winter, I have been thinking on this verse a lot. It is the one that inspired me to create this study so I hope you find this lesson especially encouraging.

This verse seems pretty straightforward, right? When it snows the Proverbs 31 woman is ready with red clothes for her family.

Hmmm...not quite!

As someone who enjoys making clothing and knit goods, I like this verse. To me it speaks of preparedness for the harsher seasons. I think THAT is what this verse emphasizes.

I did some research to see what else I could learn about this verse. I consulted several online versions of Biblical commentaries, and they had some interesting notions about the word scarlet used here. My first thought was that it literally meant red items, which perhaps signified a wealthy status. I know purple garments were costly during Biblical times, so I assume other rich hues (such as red) would be as well.

My research shows I am correct, but Proverbs 31:21 does not actually refer to garments dyed red. In the early manuscripts of the Bible the word used here meant "double layer". So her household was clothed with enough appropriate layers to stay warm in the cold climate.

It is worth noting that some commentaries suggested the verse was, in fact, referencing brightly coloured clothing because it is to show us that the Proverbs 31 woman wanted her family to look nice. Admittedly, I dislike this theory because I think about how my husband would rather be wearing cozy layers that are WARM instead of a few pieces that look stylish! But please don't think I am trying to twist scripture to fit my narrative of this study! We know so much about the Proverbs 31 woman already, so I think using that knowledge, we can say that her focus would be on function rather than form.

Here are some things we already know about the Proverbs 31 woman:
- she is sensible
- she is trustworthy and cares for the needs of her family
- she is diligent and hardworking
- she desires to serve the needs of her family

I can't imagine a woman who is all those things would also prioritize her own, or her family's physical appearance above practicality. Now, I do believe she would make sure everyone looks neat and orderly when applicable, but she would be more concerned with how practical each piece is, don't you think?

I believe the main lesson to glean from this passage is that we are to be planning ahead and be prepared for our climate, seasons, etc. I live in Canada where we have four distinct seasons. In the winter we have a lot of snow, so part of my preparations for the season includes making sure our winter gear is still suitable (fit, no holes, all the accessories have a pair if applicable). Of course, your winter may be different than mine but there are still ways to prepare.

For me that means keeping an eye on the weather forecast for any potential storms because we risk losing power. If that happens we would not be able to get water or cook using our kitchen stove, so I make sure we have our emergency water jugs filled and lots of wood available for cooking on the wood stove.

Do you know why the Proverbs woman is not afraid? She trusts God and knows that He will take care of her and her household. But she does not only rely on blind faith...she does her part, "using the brains God gave her" (to quote an old phrase!) and knows that she has done what she can to be prepared.

Reflection Questions:

1. If you have not already done so, take stock of your family's winter clothing and outerwear. Is it in good repair or does it need replacing? Does everything fit everyone? Do you have extra socks or mittens or any other items that tend to go missing?

2. Review the Reflection Questions in lessons 1, 2, 3, and 5 and make note of any areas you still need to work on. Commit to making progress with them. For example, if you have not started making a list of pantry essentials (lesson 3) or have not yet prayed for wisdom to prepare for winter (lesson 1), make time to do so.

Lesson 11: Verses 22

*"She makes coverings for herself;
Her clothing is fine linen and purple.
Her husband is known in the gates,
When he sits among the elders of the land.
She makes linen garments and sells them,
And supplies belts to the tradesmen."*

Even though these verses do not specifically apply to winter preparedness, they are still valuable to study. I hope you will take the time to read through this lesson carefully and think of how to utilize this passage of scripture in the upcoming season (as well as daily life!).

When studying verse 22 I struggled because I couldn't figure out any deeper meaning to the words, besides strictly physical appearance. The commentaries I read pretty much said the same, although many of them consider the word coverings synonymous with tapestries (meaning decorative hangings but also bed coverings).

If we reread the verse with that in mind it might say something like "She makes beautiful tapestries and blankets; she wears expensive garments."

While that is interesting, I have to believe verse 22 is telling us something deeper. Perhaps the point is to stress that the Proverbs 31 woman takes care of her appearance and does her best to look put together? But how does that apply if someone is unable to afford expensive clothes or the latest styles? Maybe it means she is a skilled craftswoman and can make nice decor and practical things like blankets. That does not seem likely either, based on what we learned in lesson 3.

To me, this verse means women should show their bodies the respect it deserves. After all, Jesus paid a high price for us (I know that at the time Proverbs was written Jesus had not been born yet). In lesson 7 we read about the importance of keeping ourselves healthy and in shape so we can best serve our families. I believe verse 22 here is an echo of that.

We know the Proverbs 31 woman cares about her homemaking duties, so I am going out on a limb to say that the first part of verse 22 means modern day women should be putting an effort into the upkeep of our home. That isn't to say we need to decorate in a certain style, with expensive furniture, or even be so focussed on cleanliness that we forget to enjoy our space. While it may not be realistic to have a spotless home all the time, we should be making an effort to create a happy and calming place of refuge.

Here are some practical ways to do that:

- making sure the house is picked up before your husband comes home, or before everyone goes to bed
- working to reduce clutter of unused or not needed items
- keeping things organized so everyone know where to find items (whether or not they look hard enough is up to them!)
- keeping towels and bed sheets fresh

And when it comes to respecting our bodies, and keeping ourselves looking presentable, I think it is as easy as changing out of PJs in the morning! I believe dressing well at home is important, but I think a lot of ladies find themselves too busy to put effort into their appearance. Full disclosure: I do not wear makeup or jewellery (except my wedding rings) at home. It takes less than five minutes to braid my hair or just push it back with a head covering, and then get dressed in simple clothes. I know what I wear is not particularly stylish, and I have been called frumpy on occasion. But here is the thing: I am still making an effort to look put together! For me that means having tidy hair and wearing day clothes (not pjs), which means a skirt or dress and a sweater for winter.

As I prepare for winter in my home, I am going to think on this verse as a motivator for days when I don't want to do housework or feel like staying in pjs.

Verse 23 does not really apply to winter, but it is still good for study, because our home life directly affects our behaviour. If we feel disrespected, unloved, under appreciated, etc at home, that WILL translate into how we conduct ourselves at work, school, playgroup, on errands, at church, and so on. But if we know our spouse respects, values, and loves us, we will carry ourselves differently.

We read that the husband of the Proverbs 31 woman is known in the gates. What kind of gates are we talking about here? The gates in Biblical days were the entrances into the walled cities. There was usually an outer gate, a corridor into the city, and then another inner gate. This system was meant to serve as protection from invaders. It was also a place of central activity for residents and visitors. This is where people met to conduct business transactions, where court was held, where public announcements were made, and so on.

The Proverbs 31 woman's husband is well known in this busy area of the city, and I am going to go so far as to say his wife is partly responsible. Let me explain: because of her capability to run their home, her husband is free of stress, and is able to do his part in public life. If their home environment was stressful he may be known for different reasons, such as being short with people, having a temper, etc.

Take a look at Proverbs 12:4 which says *An excellent wife is the crown of her husband, but she who shames him is like rottenness in his bones.* Yikes, I would rather be compared to a crown than rottenness, wouldn't you?

It would be prideful for a wife to think she is solely responsible for her husband's reputation, but she definitely plays a part. The Proverbs 31 woman is excellent (verse 10), trustworthy (verse 11), respectful (12), hardworking (13-15, 17), level headed (16), productive and not idle (19), and caring (20). These positive character traits make it possible for this woman to elevate her husband. When he feels valued, loved, and respected at home, that will directly impact the way he is out in society. I know that may sound trivial, but trust me on this. It is something I have witnessed personally.

Consider this verse in Proverbs: *It is better to live in a corner of a roof than in a house shared with a contentious woman.*

This is mentioned twice, word for word, in Proverbs (21:9 and 25:24). Do you think this is because it is an important thing for wives to understand and remember? I sure do. <u>Contentious</u> means someone likely to cause an argument; someone who is quarrelsome or characterized by argument. I don't know about you, but I certainly do not ever want to known as a woman who causes arguments.

Do we read anything in Proverbs 31 about being argumentative? This woman described for us is not a pushover but she respects her husband and does him good (verse 12).

The last part of this passage is often used as proof that God is fine with women having careers outside the home. I want to you to take notice of the previous verses, from 10-23. The Proverbs 31 woman has already seen to the needs of her family and household, has made wise purchases, stays busy and productive and helped the less fortunate. Only then does she work outside the home here in verse 24.

I want to make a bold statement here: I believe God is pleased by women who put their family above a career. That is not to say women should not work, but their focus needs to be on their family first, and then their job (this means something different to everyone so I am not going to tell you what to do for your own situation). I have worked full time and part time while being married, and I can honestly say that I could not work and keep house. Is that just a personal shortcoming? Perhaps, but I saw it as confirmation that God wanted me to be a homemaker. At present I have a small home based business, and of course, I am writing this book. Both of which could be considered jobs but neither are causing me to sacrifice my home duties.

The woman here has already cared for her house and family, since those are her priority, and then she goes to sell her items (which we will classify as working). She chose to produce and sell useful items (clothing and belts) that could be sold for profit or even traded for something else useful to her. She was prudent and financially wise, which we learned about in lesson 6 of this study. She is also wise with her time, and uses it productively.

I know this lesson was a bit content heavy, and I appreciate you taking the time to read through it. I truly hope it will encourage you in all aspects of life, not just for the winter season.

Reflection Questions:

1. What are some things you can do daily to maintain your home? Write them down and make an effort to implement them. It could be as simple as spending 10 minutes before bed tidying the kitchen.

2. Review the Reflection Questions in lesson 7. Are you working on health goals and a homemaking mission statement? If not, do that now.

3. Memorize Proverbs 21:9 and let it serve as a reminder not to seek out arguments with your husband.

4. If homemaking is not your heart's desire, pray that God would change that. I am not advising you to quit your job, if you have one, but I am suggesting that your home and family need to be a higher priority than your career.

Lesson 12: verse 25

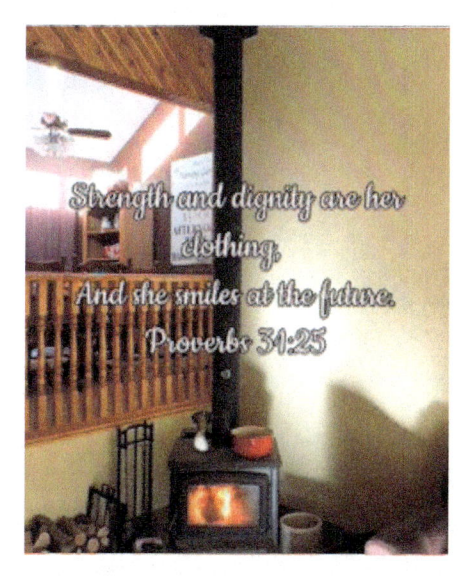

*"Strength and dignity are her clothing,
And she smiles at the future."*

We already talked about how the Proverbs 31 woman is physically healthy but I think here we learn that she has inner strength.

She is strong enough to fight against temptations, idleness, gossip, jealousy, harsh words, etc. She is strong mentally and spiritually because she spends time studying scripture, praying, living intentionally. She follows God's teaching and commands and that is why she has strength of character.

I want us all to think about secular culture says about a woman of strength, and compare that to what Scripture says. Do you think they measure up? I'd say there are a lot of differences, and we all need to ask ourselves if we want to be strong in the eyes of the world or in the eyes of the Lord.

Why would the author of Proverbs 31 say strength and dignity are her clothing? Why not say something like "she is a spiritually strong and dignified woman"? Clothing is often the first thing we notice about another person, maybe because of how much they are wearing, how little, the style, the colours, and so on. I believe this passage of scripture is telling us our strength and dignity should be so prominent that it is obvious to others. Certainly that doesn't mean we need to brag about our spiritual disciplines or call attention to ourselves, but we should be radiating Christ-like behaviours. Our inner being is more important than our outer.

Matthew 6:28-30 says *And why are you worried about clothing? Observe how the lilies of the field grow; they do not toil nor do they spin, yet I say to you that not even Solomon in all his glory clothed himself like one of these. But if God so clothes the grass of the field, which is alive today and tomorrow is thrown into the furnace, will He not much more clothe you? You of little faith!*

This doesn't mean we should not care about our appearance at all, but rather that it should not be a worry or stressor for us.

First Timothy 2:9-10 tells us *Likewise, I want women to adorn themselves with proper clothing, modestly and discreetly, not with braided hair and gold or pearls or costly garments, but rather by means of good works, as is proper for women making a claim to godliness.*

Again, the emphasis is not on what we wear, but our inner character.

Finally, in First Peter 3:3-5 it says *Your adornment must not be merely external—braiding the hair, and wearing gold jewelry, or putting on dresses; but let it be the hidden person of the heart, with the imperishable quality of a gentle and quiet spirit, which is precious in the sight of God. For in this way in former times the holy women also, who hoped in God, used to adorn themselves(...)*

This passage says we shouldn't make ourselves more beautiful just on the outside; we should desire to have a beautiful heart.

All three of these passages are instructing us not to be obsessed with the outer appearance. This is echoed in Proverbs 31:25 by saying the things that are most noticeable about this woman are her strength and dignity

What do you think it means to be dignified? Here are some ideas:

- a woman with inner peace
- someone who lives with integrity; focused on truth, goodness, and beauty
- one who respects herself in act and speech
- a woman who acts, speaks, and dresses in a manner that is worthy of the gospel of Christ
- someone who is calmly confident and restrained (the opposite would be someone who is always looking for attention or too silly)

As we enter into winter season, we may find ourselves at our wit's end. Our families may be driving us nuts, we may be stressed over all our holiday commitments, finances may be tight, we may feel like we are still not prepared for winter, the lack of sunlight may get to us, etc. Our first response may be to react sharply or say something we regret to a family member, but the Proverbs 31 woman should be our inspiration for how to manage our emotions and words.

Why do you think the Proverbs 31 woman is smiling at the future? I believe it is because she is prepared for whatever may come and is therefore not stressed. All the other verses in this section of scripture show us that she plans ahead and makes wise choices. She also knows her value as a person is not merely her physical appearance, or her accomplishments. She knows that all she does is for God's glory. Since she knows her worth is not just how she looks, she also does not fear aging (I'd like to think she is looking forward to passing down wisdom and mentoring younger women, Titus 2:5 style). Finally, she smiles at the future because she knows that this earth is not her home. One day she will be with her Lord in Heaven, and she eagerly awaits that time.

For now, she will live out His commands and teachings, strive to have a gentle and quiet spirit, work hard at all her tasks, love her family, and spread the Gospel.

Let that serve as our reminder to continue with this series and be open to learning something new.

Reflection Questions:

1. Reread the following verses: Matthew 6:28-30, 1 Timothy 2:9-10, 1 Peter 3:3-5 and meditate on them. How do they apply to your life?

2. When you feel yourself about to react without thinking clearly, bite onto your tongue and take a deep breath. Quickly pray for the words to say, and then speak.

3. What are some skills or habits you can work on that will help you prepare for winter? Write them out and make an effort to practice them. Examples include cooking from scratch, organizing your freezer for ease of storage and meal planning, knitting or crocheting warm hats, committing to regular exercise, making gifts for the holidays.

Lesson 13: verse 26

*"She opens her mouth in wisdom,
And the teaching of kindness is on her tongue."*

This lesson will expand on the previous one in case anyone needs further resources as she works on controlling her words and tone of voice (I'm not pointing fingers at anyone but myself!). As with some of the other verses, this one does not directly apply to preparing for winter but it is still beneficial to study.

I am going to break this down into two parts and talk about each one on its own, starting with the wisdom aspect of this verse. If you read more of the book of Proverbs you will see it is filled with wisdom. Does this mean we are to only speak using direct quotes from Scripture?

I do not believe so. Well, not entirely. It is a valuable skill to quote appropriate Scripture for a variety of situations but there are other ways we can speak in wisdom:

- watching our words and tone of voice
- knowing the value of words and not talking just to hear our own voice
- recognizing gossip and refusing to engage in it
- giving advice when asked but ensuring counsel does not contradict the Bible
- being measured with our words and not saying anything rashly without thinking first

Sometimes we don't realize the power of our words. We can tear someone down with a quick word, our tone of voice can convey the wrong message, or we can build someone up with kindness. That brings me to the next portion of Proverbs 31:25.

Scripture talks about kindness so much! Here are just a few verses that, in my opinion, illustrate well why kindness is so important.

Be kind to one another, tender-hearted, forgiving each other just as God in Christ forgave you. Ephesians 4:32

But the fruit if the Spirit is love, joy, peace, patience, kindness, goodness, faithfulness, gentleness, self-control; against such things there is no law. Galatians 5:22-23

So you who have been chosen of God, holy and beloved, put on a heart of compassion, kindness, humility, gentleness, and patience (...) Colossians 3:1

But when the kindness of our God and Saviour and His love for mankind appeared, He saved us, not on the basis of deeds which we have done in righteousness, but according to His mercy, by the washing of regeneration and renewing by the Holy Spirit (...) Titus 3:4-5

He has told you, O man, what is good; and what does the Lord require of you but to do justice, to love kindness, and to walk humbly with your God? Micah 6:8

Can you see how being kind is a command from God? It is a character trait of His, and as imitators of God (Ephesians 5:1) we should want to radiate kindness too.

Reflection Questions:

1. Meditate on these verses, and any others you find that speak of wisdom and kindness.

2. Ask God to show you areas you need to be more wise and situations in which you need to show more kindness.

Lesson 14: verse 27

*"She looks well to the ways of her household,
And does not eat the bread of idleness."*

What does it mean to look well to the ways of our household?

It means we are concerned with the management and atmosphere of our homes. We strive to ensure order, in the form of cleanliness, neatness, meal preparation, budgeting, social planning, etc. Our household (which does not simply mean our physical home, but also includes our family members) should be our priority above any paying job or volunteer work.

Notice how this verse says HER household? It does not say her friend's or her family's households...just her own. This is worth noting because we should be more focused on our own work than that of our friend, sister, cousin, neighbour, and so on. Homemakers now face a different world than 10 or 20 years ago with the popularity of social media. It is easy to look through a screen and judge someone or envy someone because of how her home looks online.

Older ladies, I want to speak to you for a moment: I want you especially to take this verse to heart.

If you are a mother of adult children living in their own homes, I am sure there have been times when you want to give your two cents about how they live. You may be right in your opinions, but I don't think you should be concerning yourself with how your married daughter or your son's wife is running her home (of course, there is a time and place for a mother's wisdom and guidance, but please use discretion). You may have better or more efficient ways of doing things, but it is not always appropriate to share them. Part of being an adult is learning to do things in your own way, that works best for you. As a homemaker we may find ourselves having to learn new skills or hone existing skills, and we may want to ask our mother for help. But we may also want to try to figure it out on our own. If you are a more experienced homemaker, please do your best to be respectful of the new homemaker's process. If she asks you for help, give it; if she seems to be struggling and floundering on her own, there may be a gentle way to offer help. But avoid pushing your way in and taking over, or telling her she is doing something wrong.

I am sure we have all been given unsolicited advice by a well meaning friend or family member, and maybe we are even guilty of that too. We all need to remember that our priority needs to be on our own household, not someone else's.

Let's move on to the latter half of this verse. The woman in Proverbs 31 does not waste her day. She completes her work, and is not lazy afterwards; she looks for ways to stay productive. When we are idle, it can be easier for us to fall into sin (for example: judging others while we mindlessly scroll social media or gossiping). If you, like me, live in an area that has cold and snowy winters you know it can be so nice to cozy up on the couch and do nothing. It is soft and warm, and sometimes a good book or show just seems to be calling your name. I appreciate downtime for rest or hobbies, but we need to be careful not to be idle.

Idle is defined as avoiding work; spending time doing nothing; without purpose or effect.

Here are some examples of idleness, which I will contrast with times of rest:

IDLENESS:
- staying in bed in the morning instead of getting up to start the day due to laziness
- scrolling through social media without engaging in the content (see *Note below)
- neglecting housework in favour of watching videos online or on the TV
- going shopping just to get out of the house when you don't need anything (if you are going stir crazy, go for a walk instead, take a drive to the library, or drive to a park)

REST:
- going to bed at a reasonable time to help you feel more rested in the morning
- taking intentional time to use social media
- scheduling time for reading or watching a TV show after housework is done
- spending time outside

*Note: I believe social media can be a valuable tool for learning and socializing. If we use it wisely and are mindful about it, we are not being idle. However, if we just scroll and scroll, or look at content that is not edifying, we may be wasting time. For example, if you like to read recipe posts or encouragement posts, that is a good use of time. If you like watching videos of people falling down or doing reckless things, that is an unwise use of time. Many smart phones and tablets allow you to set timers for social media apps, which may be helpful for you if you struggle to stay offline.

In 2 Thessalonians 3:11-12 we read *For we* (Paul, Silvanus, and Timothy) *hear that some of you are leading an undisciplined life, doing no work at all, but acting like busybodies. Now such persons we command and exhort in the Lord Jesus Christ to work in quiet fashion and eat their own bread.*

Busybodies are too interested in the affairs of other people; they are meddling and prying. The verse in 2 Thessalonians may have just been written for the church in Thessalonica, but there are other passages that echo this admonishment for living idly. Let's read them below.

"Through indolence the rafters sag, and through slackness the house leaks." Ecclesiastes 10:18
Indolence and slackness are synonyms for idleness.

"(...)and make it your ambition to lead a quiet life and attend to your own business and work with your hands..." 1 Thessalonians 4:11

"At the same time they also learn to be idle, as they go around from house to house ; and not merely idle, but also gossips and busybodies, talking about things not proper to mention." 1 Timothy 5:13
(see *Note below)

*Note: this verse is talking about caring for widows if they fall into certain categories. Verse 13 is specifically referencing younger widows, under the age of 60.

We can see from all these verses that idleness is a problem that has always plagues humanity. It displeases God and is something we should be actively seeking to avoid.

Sister, are there times where you are leading an undisciplined life, perhaps acting like a busybody? A busybody simply looks and acts like they are getting things done, when in reality, they are doing a whole lot of nothing (in other countries, a busybody may also be defined as someone who is nosy and pays into the lives of others). I am not accusingly looking down from my high horse, because I have had undisciplined and idle days.

Perhaps you are a very disciplined woman and you stick to a busy schedule. For that, I commend you. I hope your busyness is productive, and not just for the sake of being busy.

I also want to pose another question to all of us, myself included. Are we guilty of idleness in our speech? Do we talk just for the sake of it, do we gossip, do we lack discretion (see Proverbs 11:22)? Our hands could be busy and productive but we need to be mindful of our words.

As we prepare for winter, let us make sure we are adhering to some kind of structure for our days. We don't want to be idle or wasting time that we could be spending getting our households in order for the upcoming season.

Reflection Questions:

1. Review the Reflection Questions from the previous lessons and make sure you have completed as much as possible.

2. Prayerfully consider the ways in which you may be idle, and come up with plans for combatting it this winter. For example, if you spend too much time online while you eat breakfast, commit to leaving your phone in another room while eating. If you sit down to watch an episode of TV but find yourself watching multiple, set a timer or resolve to only watch at a certain time of day.

Lesson 15: verses 28-31

*"Her children rise up and bless her;
Her husband also, and he praises her, saying:
"Many daughters have done nobly,
But you excel them all."
Charm is deceitful and beauty is vain,
But a woman who fears the Lord, she shall be praised.
Give her the product of her hands,
And let her works praise her in the gates."*

When you read this verse it may be very encouraging for you, because the woman here is praised by her husband and children, and you expect yours will do the same. The words rise up here do not literally mean your children will wake up singing your praises each day. It means that as they grow up into adults, they will praise your Christian influence over their lives. Our husbands may not say the words in verse 29 but we should still be striving to bring him honour and do him good. And of course, in all we do, we should be seeking the approval and favour of God before man.

Is charming a word that you would want used to describe you? To me, that word has always had kind of a negative association. I think of a person who is self serving or manipulative, and knows how to win people over.

Of course there are people who have a natural charm and charisma, with pure intentions and lovely spirits! I found 4 passages of Scripture that talk about charm in a negative way (Proverbs 17:1, Proverbs 31:30, Jeremiah 8:17, Isaiah 47:11) and only one in Song of Solomon that uses charm in a positive way.

I am sure most of us would agree that the word used in Proverbs 31:30 is not a positive one. After all, the verse says charm is deceptive! Let's address verse 31 that says beauty is fleeting.

Whether we like it or not, our outward appearance changes over time. I wouldn't want anyone to think that aging lessens a woman's beauty, because that is not true. Let's look to Isaiah 40:6-7 for some possible context to this part of Proverbs. *"(...)all flesh is grass, and all its loveliness is like the flower of the field. The grass withers, the flower fades, when the breath of the Lord blows upon it; surely the people are grass".*

Here we read that we aren't going to live forever and will eventually die, which is something we all know. While this scripture in Isaiah seems like an obvious piece of knowledge, it is worth reading as a reminder that our time on earth is limited. While we are here we should be focused more on our spiritual growth than our outward appearance. We can reference 1 Peter 3: 3-5 for what we can focus on instead of just how we look.

"Your adornment must not be merely external-braiding the hair, and wearing gold jewelry, or putting on dresses; but let it be the hidden person of the heart, with an imperishable quality of a gentle and quiet spirit, which is precious in the sight of God. For in the way in former times the holy women also, who hoped in god, used to adorn themselves (...)"

It is worth noting that scripture does not tell us to put zero effort into our looks, but it does emphasize that our inner spirit must be more important.

What does it mean to fear the Lord? Are we supposed to be afraid of Him and His wrath? I have always understood this term to mean we should have a holy respect for God and desire to live a life that is pleasing to Him. Receiving praise for our good works or our relationship with God is not something we should strive for. In Galatians 1:10 we read *"For am I now seeking the favour of men or of God? Or am I striving to please men? If I were still trying to please men, I would not be a bond-servant of Christ."* We know the Proverbs 31 woman has children, so I think that she will be praised in a subtle way, because she raises up young people who chose to follow God. Her influence over her family is powerful and she does all she can to model Christ like behaviour to them. THAT is how she is praised! Not with accolades or recognition, not with a special ceremony at church, or a photo tribute to post on social media. She is praised in the legacy of faith she imparts onto her children and future generations.

CONCLUSION

It is my greatest goal in life to have a family tree rooted in deep faith of the Lord and a desire to serve Him. But in case you didn't know, at the time of writing this, I don't have any children (and I might not ever). That does not mean this verse doesn't apply to me though. I can still be a light for Christ in my family and friend relationships. I have been writing a blog for years, and it is my hope that I encourage other ladies to strengthen their personal connection with God. I don't write to be told how great I am; I write to point others to how great GOD is!

If you are a woman who has read Proverbs 31 and felt like you can't measure up, let me remind you that the woman described here was not someone who lived and breathed. This description was written as a sort of checklist for a man as he looked for a wife. Nowhere does it say the Proverbs 31 woman would do all these things (looking for wool and flax, working with her hands, bringing food from afar, rising at night, considers and buys a field, plants a crop, helps the needy, and so on) in one day, one week, or even a year. The Proverbs 31 woman lives a lifestyle of preparedness, productivity, love, wisdom, and so much more. This is a way of life, not a daily to do list. If you are in a season of life that has you very busy with babies or young children, or perhaps you are experiencing chronic illness or pain that leaves you resting most of the time, please do not feel discouraged. You can still implement Proverbs 31 in you life, so I suggest praying and asking God to show you how.

Oftentimes the Proverbs 31 woman is disliked because she seems like an unattainable goal. She does so much, she is so productive, her kids and husband clearly adore her, etc. Some ladies have told me this passage is not relevant for us today because all that the Proverbs 31 woman did is unrealistic. She has servants or attendants, and they may be doing the bulk of her housework for her! I certainly don't have a housekeeper or private chef or personal shopper, and I'm sure you don't either. I don't want to sound harsh, but to me, that is not an excuse to ignore the wisdom in Proverbs 31. It doesn't take servants to:

- be excellent (verse 10)
- be trustworthy (verse 11)

- be diligent and serve our family using our unique abilities (verses 13-14)
- intentionally run our household and meet our families needs (verse 15)
- be a hard worker and make wise choices (verses 16-18)
- be humble and and willing to do tasks we don't have to do (verse 19)
- have a willingness to serve others (verse 20)
- be prepared and trust God to meet our needs (verse 21)
- respect ourselves and our home (verse 22)
- affirm and build up our families and create a positive home environment (verse 23)
- make our family a priority over our career (verse 24)
- be strong and dignified, trusting our future to God (verse 25)
- speak with wisdom and kindness (verse 26)
- be disciplined and intentional with our time (verse 27)
- seek God's favour above all else (verses 28-29)

For us who desire to prepare for winter the way the Proverbs 31 woman might, we have to remind ourselves that it is okay not to check everything off the Reflection Questions lists. Goodness, we don't even have to attempt the Reflection Questions if we don't want to! I certainly recommend it though, as it is helpful for goal setting and tracking progress.

We also need to give ourselves grace if we had big plans to be fully prepared for anything winter throw at us, only to fall short of that. It is important to prepare, but also important to recognize that we always have room for growth and improvement.

It is my prayer this study encourages and educates you. I do not write from a place of knowing everything or being the authority on preparedness. I know living like the Proverbs 31 woman is a life-long endeavour and I do my best. May God bless you as you work towards preparing for winter like the Proverbs 31 woman.

with love,
Christina

Printed in Great Britain
by Amazon